THE HAS-BEENS CUP

BASED ON A TRUE STORY OF
GOLF, BASEBALL AND CHAMPIONS

JUDY CORCORAN

Published by Gray Productions
New York, New York

D1280334

This book is dedicated to my father, Fred Corcoran, who created and lived the story, and to my mother, Nancy, who was always there for him.

From the Author

THIS IS A STORY BASED ON TRUE EVENTS WITH FRED Corcoran, who devoted his life to promoting golf around the world, and the many golfers, baseball players, and sports writers he worked with. As with many stories, a few dates were changed and a few composite characters exist. It is written and presented here as a "treatment" for a screenplay. A fun movie about competition and friendship can be found in this golf and baseball story. If you know anyone who would like to write the screenplay, please contact me. And please help keep the tale of the "Left-Handed Has-Beens Golf Championship of Nowhere in Particular," the story of Ty Cobb and Babe Ruth's historic golf match and the growth of golf in America alive.

Special thanks to Tom Stanton, who wrote *Ty and The Babe: Baseball's Fiercest Rivals: A Surprising Friendship and the 1941 Has-Beens Golf Championship,* for his help.

THE DYNAMIC AND CHARISMATIC FRED CORCORAN HAD jumped at the idea of building the business of tournament golf in 1938 when the Professional Golfers' Association hired him to be their first tournament manager. At the age of 33, his enthusiasm for the game was unparalleled and as the sport's front-man, he took to the road like a politician seeking office, inviting business men, women and babies to follow him to the nearest course and witness the pleasure he lived. He was also an idea man with a keen eye for spotting raw talent, a knack for developing lasting business relationships, and a penchant for telling entertaining, behind-the-scenes stories. But he hadn't imagined the uphill climb he would have, like a caddie with a bag of lead clubs on rainy day, to get the tour off the ground. And by the spring of 1939, he had had enough. He needed a break.

It wasn't so much the combative PGA management and its fledgling tour that frustrated him, or the difficult equipment manufacturers, the demanding sponsors, and the sometimes-ungrateful pros. It was the press. Not the golf writers; he loved them and they loved him. He was famous for seeding them with stories about the players, the course, and the history of golf, especially when foul weather halted play and everyone headed to the bar for lack of anything else to do—and anything to write about.

Fred's beef was with the editors, newspaper publishers, magazine owners, and the radio producers who felt that golf just wasn't newsworthy and didn't rate a spot on the front page of the newspaper. Or even at the top of the sports page. Sure, they'd list the winners of a tournament in a local paper, and they'd published an article about a flamboyant player or a particularly challenging come-from-behind victory, but there were no spectacular headlines or extra-extra-read-all-about-it editions in golf, and warranted or not, he wanted one. He imagined golf in the headlines of the every newspaper in America. He wanted golfers to be celebrities. He created sensations and wanted a room to come alive when a golf champion entered.

To Fred, golf was the greatest sport in the world. The rich green color of the grass juxtaposed against a bright blue sky made his blood flow. He lived to whack drives with all his might, to chip on to the green with a delicate swing, and putt with precision across a terrain that could only be read at ground level. He longed for the twist and turns of each individual course, found intrigue in the unique placement of each sand trap and beauty in its ponds and streams, all of which became hazards once play began. And he loved what a challenging, gentlemanly sport it was. But sadly, and in fairness to his frustration, most Americans weren't interested in the royal and ancient Scottish game.

Having started as a caddie at age nine, Fred had worked for the USGA, creating its leaderboard system with colored crayons and butcher paper, assisted the great golf architect, Donald Ross, and devised a nationwide system of handicapping so that great and not-so-great players could compete together in tournament play. And now in his position as the first Tournament Director of the PGA, he was tasked with promoting golf to both businesses and spectators in a post-depression, pre-war United States. Only he couldn't get the publicity he felt the sport deserved and this frustrated him to no end.

Fred was a man's man, and along with golf, he followed baseball. Hailing from Boston, he and his brothers had hawked peanuts at Fenway Park as kids when they weren't caddying or selling newspapers. Fred, at age ten in 1915, had the illustrious fame of getting a black eye from the efforts of the great Ty Cobb, when Cobb hit a foul ball into the stands behind third and as a dozen people reached for it, one man's elbow went smack into Fred's cheekbone, crashing his peanut box to the ground where it, in the middle of all this confusion, landed on top of the ball.

Fred also loved boxing, a true man's sport. With an upper cut to the chin, a dance along the ropes, and nowhere below the belt, boxing, like golf, had nothing to do with a team. It was all about the man. The winner. The best. The champion of the world. And Fred loved champions.

"Would you like another?" the bartender asked as he

wiped the mahogany bar with a damp towel.

"Why not," Fred replied, pulling some money from his pocket. "Do you follow golf? You know, there's a golf tournament coming through here in a few weeks."

"No, sorry," the bartender replied. "I don't know much about golf. I'm a baseball fan."

The PGA Tour in those days was like a traveling circus, and Fred Corcoran was its ringmaster, the go-to guy, the Master of Ceremonies, the advance man, the one who made it all happen. It was Fred's job to pre-sell the golf tournament to the local chamber of commerce, telling them that his 100 golfers would need food and hotel rooms, transportation, and whiskey, of course. And they would have wives and girlfriends with them who wanted to shop and have their hair done. And they would buy gas and do laundry, except for champions like Walter Hagen, who would send his clean clothes on ahead so they'd be waiting for him in the next town.

Fred would also tell the boys at the town's bank that because he needed hundreds of scorekeepers and marshals to control the crowds on the course, he would bring in a charity and promise them a big donation for their support. Eager to hitch up to the spectacular gravy train, the charity would provide him with local people who, in turn, would also spend money in the town, eating, drinking, shopping and buying newspapers. It was one of the first win-win-win situations between professional sports and cause marketing.

"You don't know the names of any golfers?" he asked.

The bartender kept wiping the bar. "Maybe that guy Walter Hogan."

"Hagen. Walter Hagen and Ben Hogan."

"Yeah, that's it. The flashy guy came in here a few nights ago. I heard he's good."

"Good? Why he's a champion! People pay to watch Walter Hagen play golf."

The bartender shrugged as he straightened the equipment on his bar. "A champion, huh?"

"The best," Fred continued.

"Will he be playing in this tournament?"

"Sadly, no, which is part of my problem tonight. The galleries want to see the champions play, not the young no-name pros." He took a long sip of his drink. "Give me a champion on the right side of the road, all by himself and playing the course, and 143 nobodies on the left side, all playing each other, and the crowds will follow the champion."

And he was right. In golf, boxing and a few other sports, people love the one-and-only, the world's greatest, the first-to-ever, the last appearance of, the comeback, and the match to determine the crown. It was human nature. And golf was different from team sports where everyone had to pull together. Golfers were by themselves in their victories and alone in their losses.

"And I guess the weather doesn't help, either," the bartender concluded, as someone entered and loudly collapsed an umbrella.

Fred took a sip of his drink and winced. "Yes, rain is my enemy."

"Are you here for golf or baseball?" the bartender continued, knowing that the first induction ceremony of the Baseball Hall of Fame would commence in the morning.

"Both," Fred answered. "And I must tell you that I find your fine town of Cooperstown very welcoming."

"Good," the bartender added. "I'm from this place and I'm happy when I hear people like it. Excuse me," he said as he turned toward a man who had just entered the bar.

"I'm looking for a guy named Corcoran," the man said loudly from the other end of bar, which caused Fred look up.

"Why Mr. Cobb, hello," the bartender said with reverence.

Tyrus "Ty" Cobb dominated baseball and the Detroit Tigers from 1905 until his retirement in 1926. Often described as scrappy, ingenious, diligent, industrious and vigorous, he was also called the greatest baseball player who ever lived. He held 90 records, including the highest career batting average, most batting titles, most hits, and most runs batted in. He led in most games played and most times at bat, with 3,035 games and over 11,400 at bats, and he stole nearly 900 bases, including home plate 54 times.

But Cobb also had a reputation as a fighter, not because he occasionally punched people in hotels and back alleys, which lots of men did in those days, but because he played the game with both mental and physical tools. It was almost as if he deliberately tried to seem a little unhinged to intimidate his opponents.

"I'm Fred Corcoran," Fred said, jumping from his seat, immediately recognizing the baseball great, and making his way toward the end of the bar.

"Someone told me," Cobb said, extending his hand to shake, "that you're 'Mr. Golf,' and that if I need anything to do with golf, I should call you."

Fred's smile lit up his round face, accentuating his Irish green eyes. "Why, thank you, Ty. I've heard that you've seriously taken up the game. How can I help you?"

"I want to play in the Pro-Am at the Oakland Open next month. Can you arrange that for me? I don't know anyone there."

"No problem. Just give me your phone number and I'll set it up for you." He pulled a pen from his pocket and took a clean cocktail napkin from the stack on the bar. "And please, let me buy you a drink. What's your pleasure?" Fred motioned to the bartender.

"I'll have a beer," Cobb told him, "but can you put it in a paper cup? You know, one of those cups you use for coffee to-go."

"No problem," the bartender said, shrugging. He had heard much stranger requests in his life.

The two men sat at the bar together for the next two hours, talking, drinking and thoroughly enjoying each other's company. Fred found Cobb interesting, unassuming, dignified and humble. Ty found Corcoran smart, funny, and honest despite a bit of the blarney in him. Of course, the conversation got around to the storied rivalry between Ty Cobb and Babe Ruth, who would also be inducted to the Hall of Fame the next day.

"Ruth didn't get as many votes as I did, you know," Cobb told Fred, reminding him that he received the most votes of any player on the inaugural Baseball Hall of Fame ballot, garnering 222 out of a possible 226 votes. "I used to think Ruth was a circus freak but I have to admit that he showed some real talent on the field."

"Still comparing yourself to him?"

"That rivalry is a little overblown," Cobb said, waving Fred off. "The thing is," he continued, "baseball is a red-blooded sport for hot-blooded men. It's no pink tea, and mollycoddles had better stay out. It's a contest and everything that implies—a struggle for supremacy, a survival of the fittest."

Fred thought about the irony in his words. "I haven't had the pleasure of meeting Ruth yet," Fred said, knowing that the Babe had also taken up golf since retiring from baseball. He was now about 40, junior to Cobb's 50. "But I expect I'll run into him soon. I wonder," Fred paused a moment. "Do you think you could beat Ruth at golf?"

"I can beat him at anything," Cobb shot back.

"Say, I have idea. Why don't you and Ruth face off on the golf course to settle your baseball rivalry once and for all?"

Cobb took a last sip of his beer and examined the empty paper cup. "I use these, you know. I practice putting into them. But then I get mad and end up stomping on them. So now, whenever I can, I get another one."

Fred shrugged. He, too, had heard stranger things. Then he continued. "Forget being the best at baseball. Your games were too different to compare. The history books will tell the story and the statistics will stand the test of time. What you need to do is take him out right now, beat him fair and square on the golf course."

Cobb let Fred's words swirl in his brain.

"Just say the word and I'll set the whole thing up. Do you think you could beat him?"

"At anything," the tiger in Cobb snapped.

"Why don't you challenge him to play," Fred said, asking

the bartender for a pen and paper. "Write him a note and I'll make sure he gets it. I'll set it up for charity."

Cobb scribbled a few words on the paper and folded it and handed it to Fred as he got up, slapped Fred lightly on the back, and said good night.

"Are you done here, Mr. Corcoran," the bartender asked.

Fred tucked the paper in the pocket of his suit. "I think we've just begun."

FRED WAS WAITING AT THE CRACK OF DAWN IN THE LOBBY OF A forgettable hotel, having foolishly promised the local chamber of commerce that he could deliver a dozen golf pros for breakfast as part of promoting the 1939 Oakland Open. That's when he spotted a tall, athletic-looking young man arrive.

"Are you a golf pro," Fred asked him, noting that he looked a little lost.

"Yes, sir, I am," he said with a drawl. "I'm Sam Snead and I heard there was a free breakfast. But this only my second week on the tour, and I'm not sure where I'm supposed to be."

"Well, it's my second month on the job of managing all of you young fellas, and I should have known better than to guarantee anyone of anything, especially before seven in the morning. I'm Fred." They shook hands. "And it looks like it's just you and me, so let's go. You won't be sorry."

Sam hesitated a moment. "Can you tell them I'm from White Sulfur Springs, West Virginia. They pay me $45 a month to represent them."

"I'll tell them whatever you want me to," Fred said, putting his hand on Sam's shoulder like they had known each other forever, and not knowing whether or not this kid from West Virginia could even sink a putt.

Sam went on to win the tournament that week, pocketing $1,200, more money than he had seen in his life. Fred had been able to secure a total purse of $12,000, which put the tournament in the black and gave him hope. His battle was often between the equipment manufacturers who wanted the big guns to play exhibition golf instead of tournament golf and the local tournament sponsors who wanted the champs to square off at their specific event. Fred was trying to hitch up all the pros to his wagon and hoping to drain the well of exhibition golf. To help do so, Fred asked the PGA if he could sign on as Sam's manager, giving him a rising star to parade around in the name of golf, in addition to his tournament duties. They said yes, Sam said yes, and one of the first sports management relationships was born.

As Sam was leaving the hotel the next morning, he ran into Fred, chatting with some golf writers in the lobby of the hotel.

"Sam, look at this!" Fred said, pulling a *New York Times* from under his arm and flipping to the back of the paper. "It's a picture of you."

Sam leaned in a looked at the small photo closely. "Well, that's me alright." He looked at the front of the paper. "In the *New York Times?*" He removed his straw hat and scratched his head. "How'd they get my picture? I ain't never been to New York."

Fred and the golf writers had a field day with that.

Sam quickly embraced the tour, traveling by car and train to city after city, month after month, and by the time they wound up in Knoxville, Tennessee, he told Fred he was tired.

"But you're going to play this tournament, right?" he asked.

"I'm not so sure," Sam answered. "Why look at the measly little pot. The whole thing is only $3,000. So even if I win this tournament, I'll only take home $700."

"Seven hundred dollars is a lot of money to a lot of people," Fred countered. "Listen, play this tournament for me and I'll make it worth your while." Reluctantly, Sam agreed, and he went on to win the tournament by two strokes.

As he stood around the 18th green at the awards presentation, one of the golf writers, prompted by Fred, asked what he was planning for his $700 winnings.

"Ah," Sam replied humbly, "I guess I'll do the same with it. I give it to my Mama who puts it in a tomato can and buries it in our back yard."

Just then, Fred appeared with a bushel basket of 14,000 nickels. "Sam, your Mama is going to need a lot of cans for all these coins." By seven that evening, every reporter within a hundred miles was on the phone, filing this story, which very few people would read as it was buried in the paper.

"We're flying to Chicago in the morning," Fred told

Sam that night, "in a special charter plane! So get a good night's sleep."

WHEN FRED AND SAM ARRIVED AT THE AIRPORT, THEY EACH had second thoughts about climbing aboard the airplane. First off, the pilot was wearing a Yankees cap, not a good sign for a life-long Red Sox fan. And blue jeans, something golfers never wore. Golfers dressed like gentleman, and acted like them, too. At least on the course. Golf is a game where men call penalties on themselves, even if no one else saw the player make the infraction. There was an honor among them. Unseen by anyone at the 1925 U.S. Open, the great Bobby Jones accidentally moved his ball and called a one-stroke penalty on himself, going on to lose the match the next day. When sportswriter O.B. Keeler wrote about his sportsmanship, Jones shrugged it off by replying, "You might as well praise me for not robbing banks."

The pilot of the plane approached Fred, asking if they were ready to go. "And where exactly are we going?"

"Chicago," Fred said. "You know how to get there, right?"

"Sure do," he said, as he pulled a folded Shell Oil map from his back pocket and slapped it against the palm of his hand. "I got it covered."

"I gotta be honest with you, Fred," Sam said, turning his back to the pilot. "I don't feel too good about this guy. I ain't going."

"Oh yes we are," Fred countered. "We need to get on the plane and not worry about a thing."

"No," Sam backed away. "You ain't even told me who I'm playing in Chi-ca-go."

"Oh, sorry about that. It's a driving exhibition. It will be fun, and you don't even have to play a round if you don't want to," he said, picking up Sam's golf bag like a pro caddie. "Have you heard of Wrigley Field? Where the Chicago White Sox play?"

"Not really."

"Well, they just put up this fancy scoreboard some 400 feet from home plate, and there's a big argument going on about whether or not a baseball player will ever hit it. Could Babe Ruth hit it? Could Ty Cobb smack it? That young kid, Ted Williams, will he hit it? Well, you know what, Sam, you're going to hit it."

Sam stared at him blankly.

"Before the game starts, you're going to take out your driver, stand at home plate, take a practice swing, and hit that mother board 400 feet away with a golf ball."

"Four hundred feet?"

"Yes, not yards, feet! Why, you can hit that with your eyes closed!"

Sam thought a minute. "Do I have to close my eyes?"

"Get in the plane," Fred demanded. "I see the pilot has the map laid out on the cockpit floor. I'm sure we'll get there ahead of schedule."

At six o'clock that evening, right after the White Sox left the field from warming up and before the singing of the national anthem, the stadium announcer collected the attention of the crowd. Fred had arranged for his new friend, an up-n-coming comedian named Bob Hope, to introduce Sam. Hope was a huge golf fan who had just signed a deal for a movie in Hollywood but was happy to fly in for the event.

From the dugout, they watched as a group of batboys set up a microphone at home plate, along with a Sam's golf bag and a bucket of balls. Then Fred, Hope and Sam, who carried a bat with him, all walked out together. Hope took the mic and told a few baseball jokes and then a few golf jokes before introducing Sam as the greatest golfer alive.

"What exactly are you going to do here tonight, Sam?"

"Why I'm going to hit that brand new scoreboard out there," Sam said with an increased Southern drawl, and pointing with the bat.

"But that scoreboard is 400 feet away! No ball player will ever hit it and you think you can?"

Sam took a few swings of the bat like a seasoned pinch hitter and then switched his direction and swung it like a golf club. The crowd roared as Hope egged them on. "Do you think he can hit the scoreboard? Let's hear it!" Another roar came from the crowd. "Who thinks he can't?"

A cacophony of whistles, boos and cheers ensued.

Fred turned to Sam's golf bag and withdrew a driver and handed it to Sam as Hope retrieved the bucket of balls and teed one up directly behind home plate. Sam stepped up and took a few practice swings as the crowd grew silent. He then addressed the ball, looked at the scoreboard, and looked down at the ball as he took his swing, and with a loud crack, sent the ball to the middle of the scoreboard. It hit it with a pop, and bounced back into the outfield.

"Do you want me to hit the word Chicago?" Sam asked Hope into the microphone for all to hear.

He then set up five balls a few inches apart and drove them in a rapid-fire motion, so that the fifth ball was launched before the first one had stopped rolling. Then he buried one ball into the dirt and placed a second on top of it and struck both, causing one to fly toward the pitcher's mound and the other, to bounce up so he could catch it in his shirt pocket. The show went on for about thirty minutes, with Sam bouncing twenty more balls off the scoreboard to 35,000 hoots and hollers before they took their bows and left the infield.

The event was a huge success and afterwards, Fred and Sam feasted at a nearby restaurant. Sam, who was not much of a drinker, wanted to head back to the hotel after dinner, but Fred pleaded with him to come to the bar. "It will be fun," he promised.

"Just like that airplane ride you took me on," Sam returned. "My knuckles are still white. You're lucky I could even grip a club tonight."

"Well, you did good, kid, thanks," he said, giving him a fatherly slap on the back. "But it's important that you come to the bar and see who's there. If anyone ever calls me to give a commencement address," he went on, "my message to the youth of the world would be summed up in one simple phrase: Be where the action is. No man has ever met his destiny crying over a lonely beer at a kitchen table, and you'll never hear opportunity knocking above the sounds of trees in a forest. You've got to see and be seen. You gotta go where the people are, and you need to talk to them, listen to them, disagree with them, and sometimes, even argue with them."

"I'm about to argue with you, but I know you'd throw nickels at me or something."

About twenty minutes after they arrived at the bar, Babe Ruth, the Sultan of Swat, walked in. "Where's that guy Snead," he said loudly, as all the heads turned to identify that booming voice. "I woulda been at the game tonight but the damn weather made my plane late. Wha'd I miss?"

Fred, being the publicity guy he was, immediately introduced himself and invited the Bambino to join them, ordering another round for everyone and a Coca-Cola for Sam. And before they knew it, Sam was giving Babe a golf lesson, using a fork as a driver to illustrate his grip, and Babe was swinging a knife like a bat, until someone brought him a broom, which Sam used to putt olives into an old-fashioned glass.

Fred found Babe to be everything he thought he would be: blustery, profane, loud and a hell of a good time, laughing and joking as he played. In his prime, which spanned the 1920s, Ruth personified the "Roaring Twenties," the rags-to-riches dream, the life-of-the-party, live-for-the-moment kid. He was a very recognizable figure, drawing unsolicited oohs and ahhhs for simply walking down the street. People lit up with his wide smile, his boisterous laugh, his barrel-chested profile, topped with his wavy, dark hair.

Ruth played golf often—always for fun, frequently for money. Though golf sometimes frustrated him, causing him to shout obscenities at himself, he loved the game and was known as a solid player, hitting the ball down the center of the fairway, fairly far, and with a controlled swing that rarely led him to trouble. Since his retirement, he had taken refuge on the course.

By midnight, Fred, Sam and the Babe returned to their hotels but met early the next morning for a round of golf. A small group gathered as the threesome teed off and by the time they birdied, parred and bogeyed the 18th green, the crowd was sizable, all seeking Ruth's autograph.

"Hey, Babe," Fred said before walking off the green. "Why don't you come with us. We're headed for Augusta."

"I'd love to, but I have some business here in Chicago. But call me anytime. I'll play anywhere I can. If it wasn't for golf, I think I'd die of boredom."

"You got it," Fred said, turning away and then back again. "Oh, Babe, I almost forgot." Of course, he hadn't forgotten anything. This was part of his plan. He pulled a paper from his pocket. "About a year ago, a mutual friend asked me to give you this note. Let me know what you think. My number is on it." He turned to Sam. "Let's go, our chariot awaits."

"I thought you said we were flying back on a real plane," Sam said. "I'm not riding to Georgia in no horse-pulled chariot."

"Relax," Fred consoled him. "I haven't steered you wrong, yet."

"PUT YOUR SHOES ON," FRED TOLD SAM SNEAD AS THE PLANE took a bounce mid-flight.

"Why?" he asked like a teenage boy.

"Because you're a professional golfer."

"What's that got to do with anything," Sam said, downing a Coca-Cola. "I've played some of my best golf barefoot. Why, back in West Virginia, half the town doesn't have shoes."

"I don't doubt that," Fred said, "but we're going to Augusta, to the most prestigious event on the tour, and we golfers dress well, and don't act like hillbillies on airplanes."

In those days, air travel was so special that people dressed up for the flights. Except for Fred who didn't need a plane ticket to don a tie and jacket. Whether on the course or hustling the players to the press tent or holding court in the clubhouse afterwards, Fred was always dressed for the business of golf.

Some called golf "stuffy," which it was, and a game for the rich, which it sort of was. America in 1940 had climbed its way out of the depression and was enjoying its prosperity, a prosperity that was growing because the country was marching down the path to war, only few paid any attention to it.

But Fred didn't adhere to the dress code for the aristocracy of golf. He had learned that he never knew who he would run into at the clubhouse, in a bar, or at an airport. He was always ready to promote golf as a dignified, gentlemanly sport—and as a business.

Two days before the 1940 Masters was scheduled to begin, Fred was on the practice tee with Sam. A few reporters were milling around, trying to get a jump on who might win the championship because a lot of under-the-table betting on golf took place, especially in a town like Augusta.

As any good agent would, Fred was goading the press. "Sam is playing exceptionally well these days. Why I'm betting, if I were a betting man, and if betting were still allowed in golf," he said above the groans of the writers who each had their own horses in the race, "that Sam could win the Masters …," he hesitated a moment, sorting out the blarney and pausing for the punch line, "… barefooted!"

"You mean without spikes," young baseball-turned-golf writer Henry McLemore asked with his authentic Irish accent.

"No, I mean without shoes."

"No way!" they hollered back, almost in unison. "He'll break his toes."

"Sam, I know you can play without shoes," Fred said, hoping Sam would follow his lead. "Why, didn't you tell me you played five holes in practice in your socks before the Canadian Open last year? And you won it!"

Ignoring Fred, Sam continued to hit practice shots, with his shoes on.

"Yeah, Sam, kick off those shoes," one of the writers teased.

Fred called to Sam. "You've told me a hundred times that you used to play barefooted. So take off your shoes and socks and put your toes in the grass. Let's show 'em what you're made of."

"Fred, we know he's your boy and all," McLemore said, "but this is a lot of bull."

Fred finally pulled Sam aside and whispered in his ear. "Sam, can you do this for me please?"

"But Fred, this is Augusta. Didn't you just lecture me on the plane that I need to be prim and proper here at this dis-tin-gwished e-vent?"

Fred did worry that playing barefoot might be frowned upon at such an austere club as Augusta.

"I might get kicked out of the tournament," Sam said, driving another ball 300 yards off the tee of the practice range.

"And I'm the Tournament Director," Fred said with authority, "so take off your damn shoes and show me those smelly toes of yours again.

"Yeah," came the voice of celebrated golf professional Gene Sarazen, who had picked up on the commotion and joined the group. "Who do we have here, Huckleberry Finn?"

Ignoring his good friend Gene, Fred egged Sam on. "I'll take care of it. Don't worry. Have I ever let you down? Just play a few holes and you can put your shoes back on."

Sam finally agreed and walked off the practice tee toward his golf bag. There, he sat on it and carefully unlaced his shoes, giving the reporters a full show as he stripped off his socks and wiggled his toes.

"You know," Sam said, standing on the grass, "it sure feels good to get my feet on the ground. I really did play barefoot all the time back home in White Sulfur Springs, West Virginia. Be sure you say where I'm from," he added as he stepped up to the tee and hit a perfect drive.

Barefooted, with a gallery of sportswriters on hand, Sam teed off on the first hole with a strong drive down the center of the fairway and followed that with a beautiful second shot that left the ball about 20 feet from the hole. He putted for a birdie. He then went on to the second hole and scored another birdie, and ended the round in 68.

"Maybe I should play the tournament barefoot," he said to Fred back in the locker room.

"Oh, the press will have a field day with this. I can just see the story," Fred said.

Gene Sarazen was there, too, and the idea of Sam acting like a ruffian in a major tournament didn't sit well with him. He spoke up. "Can you imagine Walter Hagen or Francis Ouimet playing barefoot on this course?"

"Hagen would play in a bathing suit if the mood struck him, and you would, too, Gene, if you thought it would help you win. Why you played a round left-handed just to prove a point."

Sarazen acknowledged that what Fred said was partly true, remembering how that left-handed round had spoiled his game for months even though he had won a bet.

Fred continued. "Just think of the headlines: Snead puts the game back on its feet. Snead sinks a two-footer." They all laughed and thought of more jokes about Snead getting a leg up, with his feet planted firmly on the ground and a toe in the water.

"You know, Gene," Fred continued, "I'd bet on Snead barefoot over you." He cited both their records and compared them, even though Snead hadn't won that many tournaments yet. But Fred was in his element, enjoying the digs his impish humor hurled at Sarazen and proposing one of his famous fantasy matches. "Why I bet Sam could beat Ouimet. And Jones himself!" And just the fact that Fred sided with Snead against everyone drove Sarazen crazy.

"Maybe I'll do it," Sam said, entering the debate. "My shoes hurt a little, anyway."

"Noooo, you don't," Fred said. "There are plenty of things I know for sure and one of them is that you don't mix promo golf with tournament golf. Whatever you do in a practice round or exhibition is great, but you don't mess with anything during the tournament."

"And by the way," Fred added, "I'm taking you to a football game tonight to hit balls into the stands at half-time. It'll be fun. Be ready at six."

Before Sam could object, a voice from behind a row of lockers called out, "I'd like to see that."

When Fred poked his head around the lockers, he immediately recognized Ty Cobb. The Georgia Peach was born in Narrows, Georgia, and with his passion for golf, it wasn't surprising to run into him at the Masters. Having heard their conversation, Cobb played along by sitting on a bench, taking off his golf shoes, and wiggling his toes in plain sight. His legs were gnarly and scarred with shiny white dots, presumably from colliding with spiked shoes while sliding into all those famous stolen bases. Rumor had it that basemen of the time would sharpen their spikes just to injure their opponents, and especially, to hurt Cobb.

Introducing Sam and Gene, Fred invited Cobb to join them on their football trip.

THE RIDE TO THE UNIVERSITY OF GEORGIA FOOTBALL STADIUM took a little over an hour, but the time flew with Fred telling stories to Cobb and Sam, while Henry McLemore drove like the Dublin taxi driver he once was.

"How good is your game these days?" Fred asked, having yet to see Cobb play.

"It's good," he said. "Not like Sam's game of course, but for a guy my age, it's pretty decent. And I just love to play. I'm finding about 200 games a year."

"Jeeze, that's more games than in the baseball season." They both laughed.

"Ty, I've got a pro, who shall remain nameless, with the yips," Fred said.

"What's that?" Cobb twisted up his rugged face.

"It's the jitters, of the wrists. Golfers get them. It's like a slump, and just as bad. Did you ever have batting slumps?"

"Sure, lots of them. They happen when you're stoke is off. So you just got to change it up for awhile. Instead of trying to hit homers, I'd hit to the pitcher, swinging straight and short." He went on a minute and changed the subject. "Hey, have you seen Ruth play golf?"

"Why Sam and I played with him a few days ago."

"I hear he's got a wicked slice." Ty took his hands up to his left shoulder and mimicked his golf swing.

"Ah, a lefty," Sam said. "You or Ruth?"

"Both of us, actually."

"The slice is all in the grip," Sam said, giving him a quick lesson without a club. "Have you ever played with Babe?"

"No, why would I. I hear he's probably a better golfer."

"Maybe with his slice, if we get you on a long and narrow course, you'd beat him."

"I'd beat him just because I care more," Cobb sneered. "But I'd probably have to get him upset. That's how I'd beat him. I'd just get his goat." Cobb believed that the way to beat any opponent was to irritate, embarrass, dare, distract and bully him into losing his composure.

"I bet you would win," Fred said. "You know, I gave him your note."

"Yeah? Wha'd he say?"

Fred didn't want to admit that he hadn't heard back from Ruth so he just moved on. "How about I arrange that charity match between the two of you? I just know you can beat him and I know he thinks he can beat you."

Cobb looked out the window of the car before answering. "Like I said, any time, any place. Unless, of course, I have the yips. And thanks a lot for giving me something else to worry about."

Once at the stadium, Fred took to a make-shift stage at the 50-yard line and introduced Sam, pointing to him at the goal post some 50 yards away. With a spotlight shining on him, he chipped a short shot into the air that magically dropped at the 10-yard line. Then he hit to the 20. Then the 30, as a hush came of over the bustle of the crowd. Then the 40, and switching clubs, to the 50, and the other team's 40, and so on until he was hitting balls straight through the goal post, making a 100-yard drive look easy, which for him, it was.

Then Fred introduced Cobb, who stood mid-field with three bats in his hands, which he swung high from side to side to show off his still-at-his-age strength. Then he dropped two and twirled one over his head before picking up the other two to heave all three over his head. He finally selected one of the three bats.

How Fred had pulled all this out of his hat amazed Sam, who stood there, not really knowing what to do. Fred then waved and pointed to a waterboy running toward him, and Sam got the message: Chip the golf balls to Cobb.

As surprised as the crowd, Snead ducked as Cobb returned each ball with a swing of his bat, missing only one out of 20. The crowd cheered for each one.

The exhibition lasted about thirty minutes in front of a wildly cheering crowd.

"Ty, would you like to join us for dinner," Fred asked as they walked back to their car.

"Who's going?"

"Well, Henry and I, of course. I'm not sure about Sam.

But everyone is meeting at that great new steakhouse in Augusta. You know, all the pros will be there."

"You mean they all drink and eat together during a tournament?"

"Why, yes. Does that surprise you?"

"A little bit," Cobb admitted. "You know, when I started in baseball, my teammates all bullied me. It was brutal."

"Really? I can't picture it."

"It was different back then, I guess. And I was kid destined to be a star and all the old guys knew that and intentionally put me through hell. Baseball, in 1905," Cobb continued, "wasn't the business it is today. It filled with superstitions and all this weird crap like don't walk between the pitcher and ump, or don't let the ump toss his little home plate duster on your side of the field. And don't ever step on the foul line."

"So you guys didn't pal around?"

"Pal around? For most of the first year I was harassed, made fun of, yelled at, tricked, you name it. And by a clique of jealous, lousy players. It really made me mad. I had so much more talent than many of them but because I was new, I had to suck it all up. I finally knocked one of our pitchers to the ground in a hotel lobby. That sort of ended it."

"Wow," Fred replied, having heard the story but not knowing Cobb's side of it.

"And I guess a team competitive thing still lingered years later, so no, I wouldn't be caught dead with that Ruth the night before a game," Cobb said. "Or maybe I'd eat in the same room but I wouldn't talk to him. Maybe I'd even sit at the same table and give him the silent treatment. That would really get him!"

"Well, golf is a little different," Fred said, giving him a friendly squeeze on the shoulder. "We're all in this together, and just trying to get it off the ground."

"Well, I appreciate the dinner invitation but I'm already meeting an old friend for dinner."

With that, Fred offered to drop him back at his car at the clubhouse.

"So what's with those two, Cobb and Ruth," Sam asked Fred after they dropped Cobb off and continued on their drive. "Ain't they both just great players? Both in the Hall of Fame, right?"

Fred nodded. "Their rivalry exists on many levels because they're so different. To Cobb, baseball was serious business. While he was a physical player, who slid into base—and into the other team—with spikes aimed at them, he was also a mental player. He created infield dust storms while stealing bases, and slammed people out of his way while running home, but would also fake stuff to throw the other guys off. Cobb blamed Ruth for changing the game from one of skill and quick thinking to one of power and trying to knock every ball over the fence, because Ruth was all about the 'game' and the showmanship of baseball. Ruth believed baseball was something to be 'played.' His swing flowed freely and he trotted around the bases, waving to his fans along the way. Ruth became a celebrity to Cobb's mastery."

Fred was known for his encyclopedic mind when it came to golf, but also, he knew his baseball. Ask Fred his own phone number and he wouldn't remember, but ask him a stat for a golf match or a World Series game, and he was unflappable. Henry McLemore was almost as accurate and together, they were known to hustle occasionally.

"Ey, they're just so different!" McLemore added. "Where Cobb was abrasive, Ruth was sensitive, so their rivalry surprised no one."

"Cobb's possibly the best player in the history of the sport," Fred said, "even though he never took home a World Series title, and you know that still digs at him."

"And then there's the age difference," McLemore continued, "Ruth arrived in Boston at the perfect time and danced along with the team to three World Series titles in four years. Then he joined the Yankees and won another five Series titles, making it seem effortless."

"What records do they each hold?" Sam asked.

"Records are funny," Fred said. "Unless you're competing in the same way at the same time, you sometimes can't compare records. It's like comparing a Georgia peach with a New York apple."

"And if there was stat for causing bad throws, Cobb would hold another record," McLemore added. "Cobb would do crazy, cuckoo stuff. He'd slide into second, sometime head first, and then act like he got hurt on the play. He call for a time out while he got up, hopped around, winced in pain, and limped back to the bag. Then he'd signal he was okay, and as the pitcher wound up, he'd bolt and steal third."

Sam let out a soft whistle, as if to praise Cobb on his style.

"Cobb had a dozen different slides. Sometimes he'd hook his foot into base or hit it with his hips, his feet high in the air, but he was not the only one to dive with his head. But when was the last time you saw someone slide into first? Cobb did it. He even had a 'cuttlefish slide,' that would spray dirt like the cuttlefish squirt ink."

"It's a good thing we don't spike people in golf," Sam said. "And always wear shoes."

"Cobb wasn't a bad guy," McLemore defended. "It was just the way he lived and played. If you think we get into trouble these days, you should have seen the fighting years ago. It was what men did. They drank too much and punched people out. People always thought Cobb went out of his way to spike people, but it was sometimes the infielders at fault. They'd block the bases with Cobb running toward them like a locomotive. Why were they surprised when they collided?"

"Cobb did everything better than anyone else," Fred said. "He scored more runs, had more base hits, stole more bases, and had a higher batting average than anyone. And he was fierce! He would glare, scowl and dare the enemy pitcher as he walked toward the plate. And you know, Ruth hit him with a ball in the rib cage once. Of course, Ruth claimed it was an accident."

Sam nodded, "That will put some bad blood in your veins. But wait, Ruth was pitching?"

"Ruth started as a pitcher in 1914, set a record of consecutive scoreless innings that still stands, and only turned to batting latter in his career," Henry said.

"Did they ever brawl?" Sam asked, punching the air with a right and left.

"There were times when both benches emptied but neither ever struck one another, except with baseballs," Henry said. "That rib-cage pitch was when the rivalry really started, and it included everything. Like their friends. Cobb had few friends and Ruth had many, so many, in fact, that he just stopped learning people's names, calling everyone, 'Kid' or 'Buddy.' And then," he added, "there was Claire."

"Who's Claire," Fred and Sam asked, almost in unison.

McLemore whistled. "Claire Hodgeson, who Ruth married a few years ago. She dated Cobb way back."

"No!" Fred exclaimed with surprise.

"I kid you not."

"That will fuel a rivalry," Sam added.

"I'm not sure the press really knows about this. And the press has never been too kind to Cobb," Fred added.

"Cobb was vilified by the press, painted as a greedy ingrate trying to rob the team as he fought for $5,000 a year," McLemore said, "whereas Ruth was adored in the papers. Cameras and crowds followed him as he signed on for $52,000 a year in the middle of the depression, giving him a higher salary than President Hoover."

"I'd like to be making 52 big ones," Sam said.

"And Cobb and Ruth had this thing about delaying the game. Once," McLemore recalled, "as soon as the Babe stepped into the batter's box, Cobb went to the mound and started talking to the pitcher. Well, this discussion lasted so long that Ruth went back to the bench and sat down. That made Cobb furious, and when he and the others finally returned to their positions, Ruth lingered in the dugout, until the umpire finally ordered Ruth to the batter's box."

"That would get my goat," Sam said.

"And Cobb did this thing once where he tricked Ruth into striking out by faking an intentional walk," Henry continued. "He was the team's manager as well as playing outfield and when Ruth stepped into the box, Cobb called a conference with his pitcher and walked to the mound.

Ruth, expecting an outside or low pitch, stood ready to watch, when kabam, the pitcher threw a strike. Cobb ran to the pitcher all mad, like he didn't do what he had told him to, and it all happened again. This time, Cobb calls in the first and second basemen, as if to have them convince the pitcher to throw a ball, and again, wiff! He sends a strike right across the plate."

Fred waved McLemore off. "They say that never really happened. But they were famous for waving white handkerchiefs at each other from the batter's box to the outfield. Ruth would wave them back, signaling that he was going to hit a home run. Then Cobb would do the same thing but he'd bunt."

"Sounds a little show-offy to me," Sam said.

"But their rivalry was real, and there was even a time when they wouldn't pose together in pictures," Fred added. "And some of it is understandable. Cobb was famous for depriving Ruth of doubles and triples, and even a few home runs with these spectacular catches."

"It's good we don't have this kind of stuff on the course," Sam said.

"We have our own demons," Fred replied. "But the Cobb and Ruth thing was really based on competing theories on how baseball should be played," Fred said. "Cobb was all about the theory of the game. He followed Baseball Science, which emphasized bunts, stolen bases, and sacrifices. Cobb wanted to play for one run, to fight his way on base anyway he could, which meant sacrificing himself to advance a runner. It was a strategic game, won one base at a time by outwitting your opponent.

"Ruth was the opposite and his approach revolutionized

the game. He'd saunter to the plate, dig in his heels, and point to where he'd send his home run. And he was a tremendous hitter. He was all about the home runs and the power players."

"In the mind of Cobb, Ruth ruined the game," McLemore added. "Ruth hit home runs in bunches and he hit them higher and farther than any other player ever had."

Sam acknowledged the accomplishment with another soft whistle.

"And you know what," McLemore said, "I'd want Cobb on my team over Ruth. Ruth would fill the stadium but Cobb would win the game. Cobb could create more energy with a base on balls that Ruth could with a home run. Ruth would just step up to bat and knock it out of the park. But Cobb could score from second on an outfield fly, go from first to third on a sacrifice bunt, or score from first on a single."

"I just read last week somewhere," Fred continued, "that Ruth claimed he could have had a lifetime .600 batting average, but that he would have had to hit singles to do that, and people were paying to see him hit home runs."

"Well, I could shoot a 36 if I didn't have to putt," Sam said.

"Touché."

Neither Snead nor Sarazen won that year at Augusta. Ben Hogan went on to beat Byron Nelson in an 18-hole playoff, after five days of superior golf that helped elevate the Masters to one of the premier tournaments in the world and the most important of its time. The press, and the American people, were starting to take notice.

THE NEXT FEW MONTHS OF 1940 WERE RELAXED FOR
tournament golf, especially on the cusp of the war. Fred and
the PGA had proved that golf tournaments, when properly
organized and energetically promoted, were money-makers, and
sponsors were standing in line for dates. Even the government
was taking note of golf, at least, that's what Fred thought when
he got a call for Sam from Uncle Sam.

"Sam, can you meet me in Washington, D.C., on
Monday," he said into the phone, locating Snead at the Pro
Shop in West Virginia.

"What have you got cooked up this time?" Sam asked.

"Nothing really, just a round of golf with some Army big
wigs. One General and one Admiral, I think. Eisenhower
and Nimitz. They requested a round of golf with you."

"I'm not sure I want them to know where I live," Sam

said, knowing how many young men were currently enlisting. "Plus, ain't they got better things to do than play golf with me?"

"Well, they've found you. So put your shoes on and I'll make all the arrangements. Can you make it?"

"Is that an order?"

Fred laughed. "Not from me, but I wouldn't turn this down. You might very well find a draft notice in the mail tomorrow. So if I were you, I'd get myself over to that Congressional course wearing some red, white and blue. "

"What time?" he answered.

Fred was in the enviable position of bargaining from strength, but he still wanted to grow the game. He was always hearing about oddball promotions in golf with someone trying to break a marathon record of holes played in one day or someone else playing a round of golf with a whisk broom. This was strange because the game had been governed from time immemorial by rather stuffy people. Any kind of an offbeat promotion seemed especially bizarre against this classical tradition. Earlier that year, Fred had been asked by the Ripley's Believe It or Not organization to referee a two-hole match at night between two blind golfers with flash lights. He noticed how the blind men never moved their heads when they putted. He tried to get Ben Hogan to take up the stance, but Hogan rebuffed him, saying that the last thing he needed was a headline reading, "Hogan Learns to Putt from Blind Man."

Still, Fred keep an open mind and when John Cavanaugh, the hat manufacturer, tracked Fred down at the U.S. Open, Fred listened to his plea. "I want you to put on a charity exhibition for me at my home club in Norwalk, Connecticut," Cavanaugh said, "for the benefit of the local hospital."

"Exhibition golf is pretty dead right now," Fred said.

"Oh," Cavanaugh responded in a way that made Fred realize how important this was to him. "It's for a very good place called the Maternity Hostel, and I was so hoping you could do something."

"Well, let me think about it," Fred said, buying Cavanaugh a drink at the bar in the clubhouse. "The problem is that a golf match today doesn't make any noise above the regular chatter. I could get you a Hagen and a Sarazen and others, but why would it make the news? There's got to be something different or new about it." Fred was still hell-bent on coming up with an idea that would make the national news and he considered any idea worthy, as long as it was new and exciting.

"Could you guys quiet down?" Someone next to Fred called to a group in a heated exchange at the other end of the bar. "There are golfers putting right outside the door here."

Most people can't explain how they come up with original ideas but many know exactly when the ideas come to them. Fred's came to him that night as he was undressing for bed and he noticed how quiet it was. He could easily put together a celebrity foursome outside of golf, maybe with a champion baseball player or boxer, and pair each with a name legendary pro. That would grab a headline. But it didn't stop there. He recalled the conversation at the bar earlier that day with the guy complaining about the noise coming from the bar and spilling out to the course when an idea came to him. What if he were to take the game out of the library atmosphere and put it in the stadium? Instead of requiring the gallery to tiptoe around and speak in hushed whispers, he would create a hullabaloo match with a stadium atmosphere, complete with bells and whistles, boos and music.

Fred's first call was to Gene Sarazen and once he explained the idea, Gene, being one who never really got the stuffy atmosphere that surrounded golf, was quick to sign on. The next call went to Ty Cobb. Cobb would certainly thrive in a stadium atmosphere.

"You want to do what?" Cobb said as Fred explained the idea through a crackling telephone line.

"We'll encourage the crowds to whoop it up, heckle you, just as you're putting and driving. I'll get a band to follow you and play music. It will be a spectacle."

"I'd love that. You know how that revs me up. I've never understood why people are so quiet in golf, like whacking a golf ball somehow requires more concentration that hitting a fast ball. But I'm not sure I'll be back east for a while. I'd tell you to call Ruth, but you know how his game stinks these days."

Fred did call Babe Ruth, along with John "Mysterious" Montague, the infamous and enigmatic trick-shot who was an excellent golfer as well. Montague was famous for betting on anything, playing with rakes and shovels, driving 300 yards, drinking abnormal quantities of liquor, and reportedly, knocking birds off telephone lines with golf shots. He traveled in Hollywood's circle, befriending Bing Crosby and Johnny "Tarzan" Weissmuller, before an unauthorized photo revealed he was actually LaVerne

Moore, a former minor-league pitcher who had been wanted for years for armed robbery. He stood trial, was acquitted, and was now looking to make some money on the East Coast.

Ruth, now in his forties and missing baseball terribly, turned all his athletic energy to golf, telling Fred that he played more than 300 rounds of golf that year. And his game didn't stink. He was a respectable golfer, maybe even a little better than Cobb. So when Fred called, Babe joined the party, loving the idea.

Finally, Fred called Sam, who had much the same reaction as Cobb.

"What is it you want me to do this time?" he asked, and once he heard the idea, he threw his hat into the ring as well, which was a good thing, since the sponsor of the match made hats.

Fred enthusiastically told Cavanaugh about the music. "I've just heard back from Fred Waring and he's on board with his Pennsylvanians, but we'll need a truck or something to transport the band around the course."

"How many will be in the band?" Cavanaugh asked.

"I'm not sure, but count on six. And we'll need an announcer," Fred continued, thinking aloud. "I'll want him to do a play-by-play over a loud speaker, like he's calling a baseball game. But I want him to really rattle the cage and get the crowd to whoop it up. Maybe add some sound effects. Bells and whistles, sound effects, noises. That sort of thing. And you make hats, right? Can you get us some crazy hats. Like the women wear on Easter. We'll pass them out to the gallery and have them wave them when they're putting." Fred was nearly laughing as he was creating his vision on the fly.

The next day Cavanaugh called with a suggestion. "Colonel Stoopnagle, the radio guy lives near here," he said. "I could ask him to be the announcer." Stoopnagle was part of a well-known radio comedy team who were credited with being radio's first satirists.

"Great idea," Fred said. "Get me his number and I'll put it all together."

A few weeks later at Shorehaven Golf Club, the foursome of Snead, Sarazen, Ruth and Montague teed off to the strains of "Take Me Out to the Ball Game," played by Fred Waring and his combo, who had arrived from New York with trumpets, drums, a stand-up bass and saxophones, and officiated by Colonel Stoopnagle of radio fame. While part of the band marched from hole to hole in a lively beat, others rode with Stoopnagle in a sound truck.

"And on this first hole," Stoopnagle announced, "we have Gene, the mean and lean, Sarazen who plans to use a putter from the tee. What? Oh…no? He's not using a putter, he using a wedge. What? Hey can you get your facts straight. What club is he using? Someone tell me. Gene! Gene! What club are you driving with?"

The gallery ate it up, and on it went, with farting and sneezing sound effects, along with silly and absurd comments about each shot and each player and each hole.

Ruth was in his glory on this stage. While chomping on a lit cigar, he would spit it to the ground before making contact with the ball on one swing and keep it in his mouth on another. People started betting on whether or not he'd drop the cigar. On another hole, with a four-foot putt, he got down on his hands and knees and shot the ball into the hole billiards-style, using his putter as a cue stick, after chanting some mumbo-jumbo over the ball.

"Play on," Sarazen encouraged the band. "I can't wait to get my swing synchronized to that swing music!"

At one point in the proceedings, as Ruth lined up a putt, the gallery, out of tournament habit, was politely silent. Ruth turned to them and said, "How about a little noise around here? How do you expect me to putt in all this silence?" He looked around and took a practice swing, using his golf club as a baseball bat, which evoked cheers and hoots from the crowd, and then pulled a bat out of his golf bag, only to reveal that it had a putter attached to the end. After he struck his putt, which held to the lip of the cup, he clutched his heart and fell to the ground, rolling over and over down the sloped green like a bale of hay.

On one tee, John Montague had his caddie lie down on the ground and proceeded to hit a ball off the bridge of his nose. Of course, Ruth wanted to try that but got a lot of laughs when they ball kept rolling off his face and onto the ground. On another green, Montague lined up six clubs and putted his ball so that it bounced off each club like an 8-ball before sinking into the hole. And on one more green, he placed his foot next to the ball and tapped his putter so that the ball jumped over his foot to ring the cup.

With a paid gallery of 6,000, many in hats, it was a wild affair and a widely successful one—especially from the publicity point of view. What's more, Snead went around in 69, one under par, and Sarazen a 70, proving that all this tippy-toe jazz and finger-on-the lips business is unnecessary. A good golfer should be able to concentrate in a noisy factory or stadium. And Fred was pleased to see that many newspapers and magazine editors had come out for the show.

The next day, however, Fred received a long-distance call from Harold Pierce, the president of the USGA. "I hear you had quite a bit of excitement up there in Norwalk the other day," he started. "Tell me about it."

"It was quite a match," Fred said cautiously, picking up on the tone of Pierce's voice as he went on to relay the events of the day, adding his own color and commentary and acknowledging the match's promotional value and the publicity gained. He also made the point of how well Sarazen and Snead had played.

When he was done, the USGA president chuckled lightly. "It sounds like a lot of fun," he said finally, "but I hope you never do it again."

Fred heard it as an order, not a request.

WITH A WELL-RUN TOUR, FRED WAS TAKING THE GAME OF GOLF from a minor curiosity to a major business, helped tremendously by a few well-placed stories and all of his publicity events. But still, he wanted more. He wanted golf to be the talk of the town.

Back on the West Coast in the spring of 1941, during a bout of rain at a tournament, Fred was in the clubhouse with the rest of the golf writers, bantering about fantasy matches and memorable moments. He was in the middle of one of his famed stories when Cobb slipped into the room, unnoticed by the writers who were sitting around Fred as if he were the Pope and hanging on his every word. Fred was a master storyteller, known as a seanachie, the term for an Irish historian who traveled from town to town, regaling the locals with his stories in exchange for a home-cooked meal.

"And there I was at the 1930 U.S. Open, in June, on a sweltering hot day at Marion," Fred summed it up, "and I'm up on this ten-foot ladder working the leaderboard, which as you probably know, was my first contribution to the game. And there I am, not paying one bit of attention to the fact that the great Bobby Jones was completing the Grand Slam of golf by winning both the U.S. and British Amateur titles and both the U.S. and British Open titles, all in the same year. You see, I'm climbing up and down this ladder in the heat as the score is being reported to me, and I'm marking the birdies in blue and the bogies in red using wax crayons, and it was so hot that the crayons just melted in my hands. Talk about this weather! It will be the end of me."

As the group laughed and chatted to each other, Fred noticed Ty standing near the bar, drinking from a paper cup. He headed over immediately.

Without even saying hello, Cobb demanded to know, "Why do you want me to play Ruth so badly?"

"No special reason," Fred said, playing Cobb like a fiddle, "except that I know Ruth likes the game and played fairly well at the charity match last year in Connecticut." He also knew that Cobb and Ruth's relationship was amicable, but it was ripe to be presented as strained, saying that the two rarely spoke. "Playing him would settle the score between you two. You know, I've been after you for the last two years to play him. Remember that night in Cooperstown when you wrote that note to Ruth?"

Cobb nodded, acknowledging him.

"Do you remember what the note said?" Fred was convincing. "I remember exactly. It read, 'I can beat you any day in the week and twice on Sunday at the Scottish game.' Do you remember?"

"Of course I remember. I'm not that old. And I *can* beat him any time."

"So let's get a golf match together," Fred said, showing his excitement at the idea. "Will you do it?"

"Sure," Ty replied, "I'll play him anytime, anywhere, and for any amount. But you're wasting your time. I talked to Ruth a year ago and he won't play me."

"You leave all that to me," Fred said, jingling his pocket to see how many nickels he had on him. Fred knew the idea had intrigued Ruth even though he hadn't formally presented it to him.

Fred tried several times over the next few weeks to contact Ruth but never got him on the phone. Between the two of them, they were criss-crossing the country, and Fred was still a one-man show. He had no real office and lived in hotel rooms. But Fred was very determined to make the Cobb-Ruth Golf Match, which had lingered in barspeak for years, happen now. With the war breathing down America's neck, the Brits had pulled out of the game and cancelled the Ryder Cup along with the British Open so there was a mid-season lull. He needed to find Ruth!

Cobb was paired in the 1941 Masters Pro Am with Snead and Fred was once again with Henry McLemore, who was scratching around for column material. As they found Cobb at the practice tee, Fred reminded Cobb of their conversation about the match with Ruth.

"So, have you located that baboon, Ruth, yet?" Cobb called aloud to Fred, which made the heads of all the writers turn around.

"I'm working on it," Fred said, turning to the writers. "What would you think of a Hall of Fame Match between Ty Cobb and Babe Ruth? You'd like that, right?" They hooted and hollered. "I'm working on getting these two big guys together to play for charity, for the war effort, and I hope to have an announcement for you next week."

Then McLemore started in on Cobb and a few minutes later had Cobb repeating his challenge to Ruth—with fresh adjectives and some unprintable words. Fred took this as the official word and the game was on—if he could get Ruth to agree.

Fred started pulling out all the stops as he wired Ruth his invitation. Everywhere he went, he talked about the match, harping on the tense nature and bitter rivalry between the two. He told a reporter, "I don't believe there are any two other men who would draw as much attention as Cobb and Ruth. There have been 10,000 arguments as to which of the two was the better baseball player and that question never will be definitely settled. And in recent years, since they quit baseball, there have been arguments concerning their golfing skills. Now, we have a chance to settle that one."

Late that night, still worried that he hadn't been able to rouse Ruth, Fred and Henry hatched an idea. Cramped in a phone booth together, they called Western Union and dictated a telegram to Cobb.

"If you want to come here and get your brains knocked out, we're on." They signed it, "Babe Ruth." At the same time, they sent one to Ruth from Cobb. "I could always lick you on a ball field and I can lick you on a golf course.

Too scared to play me, pansy?" At the same time, they sent a dignified telegram to both of them, officially inviting them to the "Greatest Championship Golf Match of All Time."

Fred had a few regrets about his actions the next morning but knew he could pull this match off. And his apprehensions disappeared as he got to the coffee station in the lobby of the hotel and saw Henry standing there, waving a telegram from Ruth and smiling. The match was on.

Fred called Cobb and proposed they meet at the Commonwealth Country Club in Newton, but Cobb was suspicious. "Is that where Ruth plays when he's in Boston?"

"I don't think so," Corcoran replied. "In fact, I don't know if he's ever played there."

Cobb thought a moment. "You'll be telling me next that he's never been in Boston!" But the upcoming match seemed to fire up Cobb. He had been out of baseball for thirteen years and, according to some, had been a little down lately, calling himself a "has been" and "old geezer."

Fred went back and forth for weeks, setting up the match. Ruth promised that he wouldn't give him any trouble on any points, but warned him about Cobb. "It's that Cobb who'll give you headaches about the arrangements. I see he's already saying he hopes he gets me on a golf course with narrow fairways and tight greens, so that I'll be in the rough all day."

And Cobb continuously warned Fred about Ruth. "He'll demand steak and champagne for breakfast, delivered to his room by some showgirls."

Head to head, Ruth had a five handicap and Cobb, a

nine. Even Cobb conceded that Ruth might be the better golfer.

"Well, let him talk," Ruth continued. "I'll do my talking after the match is over."

And on it went, back and forth. Fred had properly peppered the press pre-match and the buzz had begun with phrases such as, "In the making for at least fifteen years" and "big and historical" and "there will be fireworks." The writers had a field day, bandying words like dynamite, showdown, historic match up, fierce competitors, explosive personalities, and to-the-death honor. The rivalry may have been designed by hype, but there was some truth to it. Both men were fierce competitors, and friendship or not, both wanted to win—badly.

With the date set in early May, only a week away, Fred got a message from Cobb, saying that he had hurt his shoulder and couldn't make the match. Distraught, he tried to locate Cobb when he got a call from a very apologetic McLemore.

"I'm really sorry, Fred," Henry started. "I was interviewing Cobb on the phone, and you know how I can be. I told him that Ruth is regularly shooting 69 and 70 and hitting the ball 300 yards and that he's mastered his short game, and Cobb says, 'Good lord, if I had known this, I never would have committed to the match. Ruth will murder me. I'm just a fair amateur player, with a bad shoulder. A really bad shoulder. Tell Fred it's off.' And then he hung up on me. You gotta do something," McLemore said.

"Yeah, I'll do something, all right," Fred fumed. "I'll do

something to you!"

Furious, Fred found Cobb and told him McLemore had made the whole thing up, that Ruth was playing like he always did, and was actually a little out of shape. "In fact, he told me that even though he carded a 71 on a course in San Francisco last month, he came back two days later with the same clubs and on the same course and shot an 84. 'That should give you an idea of my game,' he told me."

"Are you sure you're not conning me, too?" Cobb asked. "I've got a $1,000 bet on myself to win. And I'm not going out on a limb just to watch you chop it off right under me."

"You have my word," Fred offered, which, despite his occasional shenanigans and frequent exaggerations, was highly honored in golf. "If Corcoran said so," was a phrase that ended many debates and settled many arguments. In fact, it was a phrase you could take to the bank.

THE MATCH WAS NOW SCHEDULED FOR JUNE. COBB, WITH HIS shoulder in good health, arrived in New York on Monday, June 23, for the Wednesday match in Boston. Fred engaged the press that day for a few public taunts, calling Ruth several times that morning.

"You know, Fred, I had to get new shoes for this match," Ruth led on. "Yeah, with longer spikes to better defend myself from that gorilla, Cobb."

"Ah, you know we never did that," Cobb answered testily as if to set the record straight. "But I'm sure as hell bringing a flashlight with me," Cobb added, "because I know with Ruth's slice, we're going to be on the course 'til midnight, just looking for his balls."

After a few more jabs, Ruth finally took off for Boston

to get in a practice round. "I don't want that son of a gun to beat me," he told Fred in confidence.

But he only had time for nine holes. Word had spread about the match and so many people showed up for autographs and to shake his hand that he worried he'd have a kink in his arm with swollen fingers the next day. "They had me signing 'Babe Ruth' on everything from match covers and handkerchiefs to candy wrappers and lunch bags," he barked.

Ruth had also wagered on the game. "I've got a chunk of dough that says my game is good enough to top Ty's," he told one reporter, off the record, of course.

Still, Cobb openly pledged, "I'll show that Ruth how to play left-handed golf. We may be has-beens, but this is a championship match!"

Fred took Cobb to Toots Shor's restaurant that night for a good meal. Shor, a giant of a man with a tremendous capacity for boisterous affection and equally boisterous animosity, was an unashamed worshipper of sports heroes. He also held the North American indoor brandy drinking championship title and was, without question, the greatest saloonkeeper on earth. Fred knew the place would be buzzing with reporters, mainly because he had called everyone he knew and told them they would be there at eight.

Toots put them at a remote table to keep the tourists from bothering Cobb, and then kept pouring tankards of beer into them. The more they drank, the more Cobb worried about his game. "Once you start to play poorly, you get in a rut and stay there for some time," Cobb said. "I haven't been hitting the ball that well. And I'm beginning to take golf more seriously than those twelve batting titles I won."

Fred let Cobb sob on as he focused on his problems—his swing, his putting, his sand play, his hands, his hips, his head—and finally broke the spell by signalling for the waiter.

"Mr. Shor suggests one of his famous 2-inch steaks, cooked medium rare," the waiter interrupted, causing Cobb to scowl. "And may I add that I'm sorry for interrupting you two."

Cobb nodded politely and agreed to the steak. "And can you bring my beer in a paper cup, one of those to-go cups."

"Ty," Fred said, grabbing the waiter's arm before he ran off. "You don't have to drink your beer in the paper cups. If you want a few paper cups, we'll get you a few. Can you bring us some empty paper cups?" he asked the waiter and then sent him off.

Throughout dinner, Cobb continued his show of bravado but privately confessed to Fred, "I never worried before a ball game. I would just get up there and swing. But golf is different. I think it is a tougher game, especially on the nerves. Look at Sam Snead and some of the others. They play themselves dry. One bad shot and a tournament is gone. In baseball, your average might dip but you have plenty of time to snap back again. And the paycheck comes in regularly with baseball."

Cobb also had another concern that he confessed to Father O'Corcoran. "I've grown to like and respect Ruth over these past years," he said. "I'm genuinely worried that the match will bust up that friendship."

"It's a game for charity," Corcoran reminded him.

"I know, I know. But I've come to like the guy, even though," his tenor changed, "I'll do everything possible to win."

"I bet you will ... for charity." Fred tried to calm him by reminding him of this, a point the fiercely competitive star was forgetting.

"Tell me," Fred said, "I've always wanted to know. Did you ever spike someone intentionally?"

"No! I am not a spiker!" Cobb said emphatically, separating each word with a huff of breath. "I never even thought about doing anything in baseball that was not completely legal. And remember, I was not the only guy who slid feet first. And I never intentionally spiked anyone." He took a large sip of beer. "I might have aimed a little high once or twice, but that's not spiking!"

After an after-dinner drink at the bar on the way out, the two drunk men somehow managed to leave the restaurant, with Cobb's paper cups in tow, with just enough time to hail a cab and jump aboard the sleeper train to Boston as it began to pull out of Penn Station at one a.m.

The train arrived in Boston at dawn, but it was customary to let the patrons of the sleeping cars snooze until seven, when the porter made the rounds, rousing people out.

Cobb and Corcoran had opposite lower berths, and Fred was awakened by the most awful commotion in the aisle. He poked his head through the curtains to see Ty in his BVDs, his spike-scarred legs scrambling, as he chased the poor porter out of the car. He turned back, his face flushed and angry, and saw Fred. "Nobody puts his hands on me," he snorted.

Fred hurried and dressed and the two of them fled from the train to the Ritz Carlton to change before going out to the Commonwealth Country Club for a practice round. At the hotel, Ty remarked that he didn't feel too well and complained that he had drunk too much beer the night before.

"Say," he said thoughtfully, "you don't suppose that guy Shor has a bet on Ruth, do you?"

Ruth had arrived at the Ritz Carlton the day before, and after his practice round, he returned to the hotel where friends and reporters showed up in force. Ruth took a table on the rooftop bar, where he fended off taunts intended to add fuel to any fires. Fred and his brother John joined the party and kept the conversation going from baseball to golf and back again and kept the waiters on a short path between their table and the bar. John told Ruth how well Cobb had played in practice, but Ruth saw through it and tossed it back, recalling how he had thrilled a crowd in front of the clubhouse, pitching to the cup from 100 yards out.

"I put everything I had into the shot," Ruth said, "but the damned ball stopped on the lip of the cup. It looked like it was going to roll in, but that Cobb or somebody must have stuck some glue there and stopped it."

With few nightclubs worth mentioning in Boston in those days, the Ritz Roof was Boston's swankest dining-and-dancing spot. What the guests didn't know was that the owner, Ed Wyner, had set up a complete private driving range on the Ritz Roof. It had everything, including a magnificent view of the Back Bay. And having heard about the party going on, he arrived with a driver and a bucket of balls, and before another round of drinks was delivered,

Babe and the sports writers were taking turns hitting balls into the bay.

Cobb arrived later, as Ruth's party was well underway, and sat at a different table, seeming more interested in the young Cuban dancers and a hearty meal than he was in Ruth. As loud remarks were hurled across the way, it became an evening that sportswriters only dream of. Bill Cunningham wrote in the *Boston Herald*, "This is no autograph carnival. It's a golf match for blood." John Kieran of *The New York Times* wrote, "Don't stand too close!" Stanley Frank of the *New York Post*, gave it his perspective when he wrote, "Compared to Ruth and Cobb, Churchill and Hitler are old chums temporarily estranged by a slight misunderstanding."

The banter and the booze flowed for hours, and a few reporters, as they had been known to do, failed to meet their deadlines.

"I've got a chunk of dough that says my game is better than yours," Ruth shouted across the room.

"I can beat you right now," Cobb said, pulling a paper cup out of his pocket. "Get me a putter and some balls," he called to no one in particular, and before he got to his feet, someone handed him the club.

"Now put this cup over there." He pointed to a spot right in front of Ruth's chair, about fifteen feet away. "I can hit the cup. Do you want to put money on it?" he said to Ruth.

"I don't care whether you can hit a frickin' paper cup," Ruth said, kicking it away. "Tomorrow is all that counts."

Cobb heard him but didn't say a word. He walked over to where the cup was now laying and picked it up. Putting it back in his pocket, he put down the putter and turned and left. Fred watched as Cobb headed back to his room to study his meticulous course notes, review his strategy for the match, and undoubtedly, practice putting into a paper cup. Tomorrow, after all, was the match above all others; the definition of competition itself. Fred wasn't sure how important this match was to Ruth but he knew how important this match was to Cobb. And it was to him, too. If he didn't make the front page of all the newspapers with this match, he just didn't know what would.

LUCKILY, FRED HAD THE FORESIGHT TO SCHEDULE THE match for the afternoon, giving them all a few hours to recover before heading to the course. He had arranged for Joseph P. Kennedy, a Ruth fan, and Edsel Ford, a Cobb fan, to act as referees. He had also brought in Arthur Donovan, the noted boxing referee, who had officiated at many Joe Louis fights, and prepped the press, pointing to his professional expertise should tempers flare.

Cobb was already in the locker room when Babe and his entourage arrived.

"Hey, old buddy. I'm going to knock your brains out," Babe said.

"Maybe. My shoulder's been hurting me. I may not be able to swing a club. I hear you've been hitting long. Do you ever shank?"

"Never heard of it."

"And I guess you're good on those short little putts. I may make you putt out, just to see if you can hole those little four-inchers. You're used to looking at four inches, right?"

"I don't expect you to give me anything."

"Well, I just hope you don't get the yips."

"Looks like he's trying to talk me out of it," Ruth said, turning to a photographer who had just appeared. "Maybe he doesn't think he can beat me."

"Can I get a photo of you two?" he asked, but Ruth held up his hand, signalling that he wasn't ready.

"You can get one of me," Cobb said, flashing a big smile, "'cause if I had a beak like Ruth's, I wouldn't want one either. It might break your camera."

"You're so full of crap you always need toilet paper in your pants," Ruth hurled back.

With the inside tension high, no one had dared mention the outside situation, which consisted of a heavy rain, making Fred a nervous wreck.

"Rain before seven exits by eleven," Fred told everyone that morning as they gathered at the clubhouse for coffee, which, because of the rain, led to lunch. And with a nor'easter that kept pouring water on the course and blowing boughs from trees, Fred knew by one that they wouldn't get out that day.

"Can you play tomorrow?" he asked Ruth, who winced and cocked his head with a no, stating that he needed to be in New York tomorrow.

"I can't stay, either," Cobb said, making Fred wonder whether he was just keeping up with Ruth.

At two o'clock, with the pounding of torrential rain on the roof, Fred called for everyone's attention. "This is the story of my life," he began. With Ruth and Cobb sitting at tables in opposite corners of the members' bar, he pointed. "On my left is one of the world's greatest baseball players ever, and on my right is one of the world's greatest baseball players ever. Out there," he pointed to the 18th green, "we would have determined which one of the world's greatest baseball players ever was the champion golfer. But unfortunately, I think we're seeing one of the world's greatest storms, so I'm calling the match on account of the weather." The group erupted in boos. "But I promise, I will work with the tremendous Babe Ruth and the unstoppable Tyrus Cobb and the Almighty Himself to reschedule this match on a sunny day as soon as possible. Please have a drink on me and promise to meet again."

"In Detroit!" Cobb shouted.

"In New York," Ruth countered.

"I will take your recommendations under consideration and be in touch," Fred said. "Drink up, everyone!"

THE MATCH WAS RESCHEDULED FOR TWO WEEKS LATER IN Detroit and Fred stopped in Youngstown, Ohio, on his way. He had some business there and besides, he had met an Ohio woman, Jean, the year before and had had a lot of laughs with her. After he wrapped up his appointments, he took a cab to her house, remembering where it was.

After ringing the doorbell twice and starting to leave, a woman in her early forties opened the door. "May I help you?"

"I'm looking for Jean," he said politely.

"Oh, she enlisted in the marines," the woman said. "I'm her mother, Wanda."

"I'm Fred Corcoran," he answered. "I didn't know. I met her about a year ago."

"I know you, you're Mr. Golf. That's what she called you."

Fred nodded, slightly embarrassed.

"Would you like to come in?" Opening the door, she called, "Nancy! We have company."

Fred remembered Jean to be a 25-year-old knockout, and when Nancy walked down the stairs, he felt his breath escape. She was an 18-year-old beauty.

After the obligatory introductions, Fred said, "Well, since Jean's not here and I am, how about I take you two lovely ladies to dinner tonight."

Wanda and Nancy each looked at each other and then Nancy said, "I'll get my sweater," and took off upstairs.

The next day, Fred arrived in Detroit. Since it was a smaller city than Boston, Fred had made some calls a few days prior in an effort to bolster attendance. He put in a call to trick-shot artist John Montague and his good friend and magical player, Walter Hagen, to play alongside Cobb and Ruth. Hagen and Ruth were old buddies and together, had helped make the 1920s roar. Some even called Hagen, "the Babe Ruth of Golf."

With everything in place, Fred met Cobb at the airport and rode with him to the hotel in the early evening on the night before the final match. After dinner, Cobb insisted on visiting Hagen so they went over to the Detroit Athletic Club to find him.

"I'm very sorry," said the clerk, "but Mr. Hagen is sleeping."

"Nonsense!" bellowed Cobb. "Give me his room number because we need to talk to him right away."

Fred, sensing a problem, called the clerk over to the other end of the desk. "Do you know who this is?" he asked politely.

"Why of course," the clerk nodded, "but I also know who Mr. Hagen is, and I'm not letting you two up there."

"I understand," Fred said, "but this really is an unusual situation and Mr. Cobb does want to talk to Mr. Hagen, and I know them both very well so I can take care of any problem that might arise." Fred dangled his arm across the desk and gently placed a neatly folded twenty dollar bill in the clerk's hand. "Do you think you could just look the other way while I look at your guest book right there on the desk? I won't touch a thing."

The clerk pocketed the cash and walked off in the other direction without saying a word and a few minutes later, Fred and Ty found Walter's room. Cobb turned the door knob, which was unlocked, so they loudly walked in. And there was Hagen in bed asleep.

"Walter! Walter! Wake up!" Cobb shouted, but Hagen didn't move a muscle. He just went on snoring peacefully. Cobb studied the sleeper and shook his head in admiration. "There's the most relaxed man I ever saw," he commented. "See how he sleeps all rolled up in a ball? Any time you have trouble sleeping, just try it. It's complete relaxation."

Hagen finally woke up and without getting out of bed, said hello to Cobb and Fred.

"Walter, I'm sorry to wake you, but do you have any advice for me?" Cobb pleaded.

"Are you serious?" Hagen asked. "You wake me up for this?" He looked over to Fred who just shrugged, mainly from suppressing a laugh. "Ty, just keep your head down. And get to bed early."

Cobb nodded, making a mental note as if he was

listening to a priest.

"And lock the door on your way out," Hagen said. "I don't want you two coming back here in the middle of the night. I don't care what you want."

THE NEXT MORNING, FRED AROSE EARLY AND WENT TO MASS, mainly to thank God for the great weather. He didn't know if he could go through all of this again. But also, he wanted to see if there were any kids around to bring to the course. Kids always made for good photos. He found the Monsignor and mentioned the match, causing the Monsignor to scurry off to make a call.

Fred was also delighted to see that by noon, nearly a hundred members of the press had gathered in the clubhouse. Of course, he fanned the who's-the-best flames and re-ignited the comparison that had raged for two decades on the ball field and was now being tested on the golf course. In Cobb's mind, the issue had been settled a few years ago when he got 222 out or a possible 226 votes for the Hall of Fame and Ruth got only 215. Most of the press just agreed to call them, "the greatest two baseball players who ever lived."

By early afternoon on Monday, July 29, at the Grosse Ile Golf and Country Club, some 10,000 fans had arrived at the course and were wandering around, waiting to witness the big match, which was scheduled for four p.m. The Monsignor had also arrived with a group of 40 young boys from the local orphanage to appear for pre-match photographs, just as Fred had hoped.

Ruth, who was stockier but nine years younger than Cobb, arrived at the first tee dressed for the day in a collarless, white button-down shirt that had been carefully pressed and then tucked into tan slacks, cinched at the waist with a dark belt. Cobb, on the other hand, wore a white sports shirt that hung down over his pants and led to scuffed up shoes. He looked ordinary in comparison to Ruth.

As they took to the first tee, Corcoran held out a driver, pointed toward the sky. Ruth was first to place his large left hand at the base of the club and Cobb followed with his left. Hand over gnarly knuckled hand, the men inched their way to the top, until Cobb held the club. He would tee off first.

Cobb passed off the club and approached Ruth. He stuck out his hand and said, "Good luck."

Ruth, suspecting something, wouldn't shake and went to inspect Cobb's hand. Cobb pulled it back quickly and raised them, showing that he had nothing in them or up his sleeve. That got Ruth's goat.

Ruth then went to his golf bag and pulled out a folding seat that balanced on a club-sized pole with a sharp end to dig into the earth. Seeing his broad backside slip into and spill over it was a sight. "This is in case you start snailing around the course and taking your sweet time with all those extra practice swings and double-checking everything," he said to Cobb. "This guy's so slow he'd stop a funeral. I really should have brought a couch," he told the crowd.

"Grumble all you want, Babe," Cobb smiled. "I play deliberately. Oh, and by the way, I stashed some bottles of scotch in the bushes along the course, in case you get thirsty. I know you'll be in tall grass all day."

Ruth seemed to approve of that barb.

And after that, with everyone expecting Cobb to badger Ruth through 18 holes, Cobb said not one word to Ruth during the entire match.

Neither Cobb nor Ruth played great golf, but everyone watched respectfully, despite the fact they clipped innocent spectators with their drives six times between them. Throughout the afternoon, Babe out-drove Cobb but Cobb out-putted Ruth, almost a parody of their styles in baseball.

The game, which went back and forth, moved slowly, and as darkness approached, Walter Hagen jokingly lit a match to help Babe see his ball. But Ruth ran out of holes and Cobb took the match, three and two, shooting a 78 to Ruth's 81. Hagen shot a forgettable 75 while Montague, who sensed the seriousness of the match, turned in the best score, 70.

Upon sinking the winning put, Ruth turned to the crowd and said, "He's a putting fool," and then offered his hand.

Flashbulbs popped from dozens of newspapers and

Time, *Life* and *Newsweek* magazines. A few radio reporters were taking notes. And several wire services joined in, which resulted in photos of the match in hundreds of newspapers across the country.

When asked by reporters about his silence, Cobb replied, "Golf is different than baseball. You don't do or say the same things on the green as you would on the diamond."

Fred agreed, telling reporters, "I just never thought he would abide by golf's customs."

"Well, now I've got something to show my grandchildren," Cobb beamed, after accepting the silver trophy in front of several hundred of history's witnesses. The ceremony was delayed as they waited for actress Bette Davis, who was in town performing at a local theater, to present the trophy.

Ruth turned to the group and responded, "It is with the greatest pleasure that I have had the honor to be a part of the 'Left-Handed Has-Beens Golf Championship of Nowhere in Particular,' with such an esteemed partner as Mr. Tyrus Cobb. At times, we wanted to cut each other to ribbons. But I have a sincere and honest respect for Ty Cobb. Cheers."

Congratulatory telegrams poured in all evening as Corcoran, Cobb, Ruth and a hundred others all celebrated together back at the hotel.

At one point, Ruth tossed a paper cup to Cobb. "Double of nothing?" he called out.

"Not on your life," Cobb shot back.

"Please, then I could say I won the Paper Cup Championship."

"Don't make light of this," Cobb warned. "I won the

championship. You didn't."

Cobb later left for a private celebration for his longtime Detroit friends, including pilot Jimmy Doolittle, who in time would be flying missions over Tokyo, and Malcolm Bingay, the editor of the *Detroit Free Press*.

Cobb later told reporters, "This exhibition golf is far more punishing than baseball ever was. During my twenty-four years on the diamond, I was never under such terrific pressure as I was while coming from behind to beat the Babe. Maybe it was because both of us were so gentlemanly. He was awfully nice to me, and I tried to be equally so. Neither of us acted that way in a ball game."

He ended the interview saying, "It was a great pleasure to play with him and a much greater pleasure to beat him."

Later on, Cobb said the match was one of the highlights of his life. "You know," he said with that competitive glint in his eyes, "I got a special kick out of beating Ruth because I outfoxed him. I started using an iron off the tee and that bothered him."

12

"You did it!" a woman's voice sang out when Fred answered the phone the next day. While sitting on the bed in his hotel room, he immediately recognized Nancy's voice. A few months after their dinner in Youngstown, she had moved to New York and they had started seeing each other.

"What did I do?" he asked.

"You made the front page of all the New York papers with your golf match. I just got back from the newsstand and bought all of them for you. And I heard about the match on the radio this morning."

Fred sat back against the headboard without saying a word.

"Fred, are you there?"

"Yes, I'm here," he said. "I'm just enjoying my moment."

"I know! You must be so excited. This is what you've wanted, isn't it? To get golf on the front page! And you said the magazine reporters were there, too, right? You did it!"

"Yes, *Time, Newsweek* and *Life* were there. Those issues should be out next week."

Fred showered, dressed and went to the lobby bar to have breakfast, ordering eggs, toast and coffee. After, taking his order, the waiter went off to the side of the bar and opened the paper. Fred could tell that he was reading about the match and smiled.

When the waiter delivered the food, Fred asked, "Do you follow golf?"

"Why, yes," he said. "I don't play much but I want to play more. And did you read about this big golf match they had yesterday?"

The match generated news stories across the country and dozens of cities and companies contacted Fred to create Cobb-Ruth events of their own. Fred hinted at a Fall '41 tour of ten matches, and while Cobb agreed, Ruth turned it down, saying that he didn't like to travel, and he didn't feel like hopping all over the country over the next few months.

THE LEFT-HANDED HAS-BEENS GOLF CHAMPIONSHIP of Nowhere in Particular made thousands of dollars for the American Red Cross and professional golf went on to become a $70 billion a year industry with nearly $4 billion going to charity each year.

After ten more years with the PGA, Fred Corcoran managed the careers of Ted Williams, Stan Musial, Babe Zaharias, Sam Snead and Tony Lema. He founded the Ladies' PGA, the Golf Writers Association of America, and the original Golf Hall of Fame. He later led the International Golf Association, where his claim to fame, he said, was having 3-putted in 48 countries. He was inducted into the World Golf Hall of Fame in 1975 as one of the first non-players. He died in 1977 at 72 – even par, as someone remarked.

Sam Snead went on to win a record 82 PGA Tour events, including seven major titles, before passing away at 90, in 2002.

Babe Ruth developed throat cancer a few years later and died in 1948. In 1969, Major League Baseball voted Ruth as its greatest player ever.

Ty Cobb obviously treasured this Has-Beens title. It was reported that wherever he lived after 1941, he kept two things on his mantle—his Baseball Hall of Fame plaque and the trophy from this golf match. He died 20 years later, in 1961, with his reputation soured as some unflattering books and movies portrayed him as difficult.

For the rest of their years, Cobb and Ruth enjoyed a good relationship, often seeing each other at old-timers games. "I can't honestly say that I appreciate the way in which he changed baseball," Cobb said. "But he was the most natural and unaffected man I ever knew."

HISTORICAL
NOTES

- Cobb and Ruth played three matches, in Boston, New York and Detroit. Cobb won two of the three.
- Fred took Sam Snead and Babe Zaharias to Wrigley Field.
- Sam Snead was not part of the Music Match. The foursome consisted of Babe Ruth, Gene Sarazen, boxer Gene Tuney, and Jimmy Demaret.
- Most of the dialogue of Cobb and Ruth is taken from quotes and reports.
- Sam Snead wasn't called before Admiral Nimitz and General Eisenhower, but a photo exists of Fred with them at an exhibition.
- Bob Hope did not appear with Sam Snead at Wrigley Field and the year of that event may be off by a year.

- Bette Davis did not present the trophy; she donated it so it was named after her.
- There is no evidence the Cobb practiced putting into a paper cup.
- The football stadium exhibition happened in Los Angeles with Ben Hogan, not with Snead and Cobb.
- Nearly everything else actually happened, but maybe at a different time or place.

50073959R00047

Made in the USA
Charleston, SC
16 December 2015